Animal Pollinators

by Jennifer Boothroyd

Lerner Publications · Minneapolis

The images in this book are used with the permission of: © iStockphoto.com/crscredon, p. 4; © iStockphoto.com/KLSbear, p. 5; © BSP/UIG/Getty Images p. 6; © O.DIGOIT/Alamy, p. 7; © Brian Murphy/Alamy, p. 8; © Merlin D. Tuttle/Science Source, pp. 9, 10, 12; © Merlin D. Tuttle/BCI/Getty Images, pp. 11, 13; © ANT Photo Library/Science Source, p. 14; Garbutt/NHPA/Photoshot/Newscom, p. 15; © Robert Dant/Alamy, p. 16; © Rick & Nora Bowers/Alamy, p. 17; © Murray Cooper/Minden Pictures/Getty Images, p. 18; © iStockphoto.com/BirdImages, p. 19; © Edward Parker/Alamy, p. 20; AP Photo/Andrew Shurtleff, p. 21; © Bill Bachman/Alamy, p. 22.
Front cover: © iStockphoto.com/YanC.

Main body text set in ITC Avant Garde Gothic Std Medium 21/25.
Typeface provided by Adobe Systems.

Lerner Publications Company
A division of Lerner Publishing Group, Inc.
241 First Avenue North
Minneapolis, MN 55401 USA

For reading levels and more information, look up this title at www.lernerbooks.com.

Library of Congress Cataloging-in-Publication Data

Boothroyd, Jennifer, 1972–
    Animal pollinators / by Jennifer Boothroyd.
        pages   cm. — (First step nonfiction. Pollination)
    Includes index.
    ISBN 978–1–4677–5741–6 (lib. bdg. : alk. paper)
    ISBN 978–1–4677–6223–6 (eb pdf)
    1. Pollination—Juvenile literature. 2. Pollination by animals—Juvenile literature. I. Title.
    II. Series: First step nonfiction. Pollination.
    QK926.B65 2015
    571.8'642—dc23   2014017713

Manufactured in the United States of America
3-42942-17875-9/13/2016

Table of Contents

Pollination

Flowers make **pollen**. Most pollen looks like yellow dust.

These are sunflower seeds.

Flowers use pollen to grow seeds.

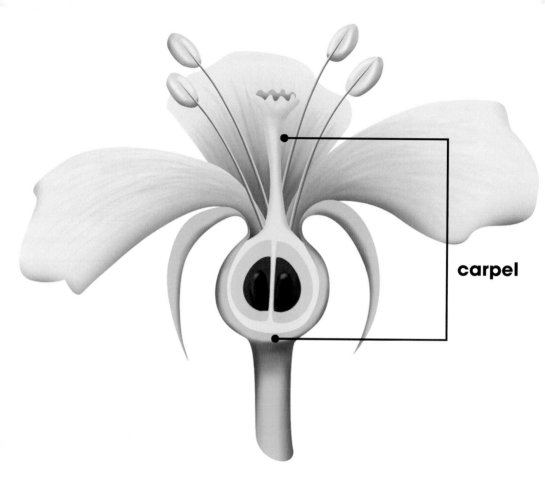

carpel

Pollination happens when pollen moves into a flower's **carpel**.
6 Then the flower can make seeds.

Pollinators help pollen move to a flower's carpel. Many animals are pollinators.

How Do Animals Pollinate?

Some animals drink **nectar** from flowers.

Nectar tastes
sweet.

Animals get nectar with
their tongues.

Bats drink nectar from flowers.

Pollen sticks to the bat.

The pollen rubs off on the
flower's carpel.

Bats are one kind of animal pollinator. But there are many others.

13

Honey possums
live in Australia.

Honey possums pollinate flowers.

Lemurs live in Madagascar.

Lemurs pollinate flowers.

Pollen sticks to
this lizard's scales.

Some small lizards pollinate
flowers.

Pollen sticks to the dove's feathers.

Doves pollinate flowers.

Many honeycreepers live in Hawaii.

Honeycreepers pollinate flowers.

Hummingbirds pollinate flowers.

Humans also pollinate flowers.

Hand-pollination can help
plants grow better fruit.

It takes a lot of helpful animals and humans to pollinate flowers.

Glossary

carpel – a part of a flower that stores eggs

nectar – a sweet liquid made in flowers

pollen – a powder made inside flowers

pollinators – animals, humans, or wind that pollinate flowers

Index